BEST IRISH
HUMOROUS
QUOTATIONS

GW00382301

BEST IRISH HUMOROUS QUOTATIONS

Des MacHale

MERCIER PRESS

MERCIER PRESS
PO Box 5, 5 French Church Street, Cork
16 Hume Street, Dublin 2

ISBN 1 85635 138 6

A CIP for this book is available from the British Library.

10 9 8 7 6 5 4 3 2 1

*This book is dedicated to the three 'Quiet Men'
– Charlie Harold, Eddie Gibbons and
Liam Ó Raghallaigh*

Printed in ireland by Colour Books Ltd.

PREFACE

The Irish have a reputation of being the wittiest people on earth and when you read this book you will soon see why. Wit drops from the lips of the average Irishman and Irishwoman as naturally and as frequently as rain drops from the heavens on the Emerald Isle. Pick up any book of quotations in the English language and you will find it chock-full of quotations from Irish authors such as Wilde, Shaw, Sheridan (R. B. and J. D.), Swift, Behan, Milligan, Beckett, Keane, O'Brien, Toibin, Leonard, Goldsmith, Joyce, Healy, Kavanagh, MacManus, Mahaffy, Moore, O'Casey, O'Faolain and Stephens. That's a formidable list by any standards. And these are just the literary wits that have left a written record of their humorous outpourings. Go to any Irish pub, golf club, school, football match, office block or factory floor, and you will hear just as good stuff, off-the-cuff and original too. What causes it and where does it come from? God only knows and He must bear at least some of the responsibility because He is probably part Irish Himself. Maybe it is something in the air, something in the water, something magic that exists in the Irish twilight between sanity and madness. Whatever the reason let us rejoice in it and enjoy one of the world's greatest free gifts – Irish humour.

JOSEPH ADDISON

1: WHY should we do anything for posterity? What has posterity ever done for us?

2: HER grief lasted longer than I have ever known any widow's – three days.

DAVE ALLEN

3: WHITE is the virginal colour, symbolising purity and innocence. Why do nuns wear black?

4: IF I got as much as £3,000 of a night's work I could do an impression of Paul Getty counting his small change.

5: IRISH humour consists of five basic themes – life, death, religion, drinking and the English.

6: IRELAND has one of the world's heaviest rain-falls. If you see an Irishman with a tan, it's rust.

7: IRELAND is the only place in the world where procrastination takes on a sense of urgency.

8: I'M an atheist, thank God.

9:   My favourite retort to hecklers is, 'If I had a head like yours, I'd have it circumcised'.

10:   My mother used to say, 'Think of the starving children of the world'.
I used to answer, 'Put it in the bloody envelope and send it to them. Anyway, they'd probably send it back with the message, "We don't like cabbage either".'

11:   I am still retired, but in order to keep myself in retirement in the manner in which I am accustomed, I have to work. It's an Irish retirement.

12:   We spend our lives on the run: we get up by the clock, go to work by the clock, eat and sleep by the clock, get up again, go to work – and then we retire. And what do they give us? A bloody clock.

Samuel Beckett

13:   Dublin University contains the cream of Ireland – rich and thick.

14:   We are all born mad. Some remain so.

15:   I am not British. On the contrary.

16:   I do not give interviews because I have no views to inter.

17: THE drink in that pub is not fit for washing hearses.

18: I'M that hungry I could eat a dead Christian Brother.

19: WHEN I came back to Dublin I was court-martialled in my absence and sentenced to death in my absence, so I said they could shoot me in my absence.

20: SHAKESPEARE said pretty well everything and what he left out, James Joyce, with a nudge from meself, put in.

21: THERE is no bad publicity, except an obituary notice.

22: KILBARRACK, over by Howth, my father always maintained, was the healthiest graveyard in the country, with the sea air.

23: PEOPLE don't actually swim in Dublin Bay – they are merely going through the motions.

24: THE first item on the agenda of every Irish organisation is 'The Split'.

25: THE bars in Dublin are shut from 2.30 to 3.30. We call it the Holy Hour. The politician who introduced it was shot an hour afterwards.

26: AMERICA is the land of permanent waves and impermanent wives.

27: IF it was raining soup, the Irish would be out with forks.

28: How about the raffle where the first prize was a week in Belfast and the second prize was a fortnight in Belfast?

29: THE Bible was a great consolation to a fellow alone in the old cell. The lovely thin paper with a bit of mattress stuffing in it, if you could get a match, was as good a smoke as I ever tasted.

30: I'M a communist by day and a Catholic after it gets dark.

31: I MET the ornithology correspondent of *The Irish Times*, a very prim and proper lady, one cold winter's afternoon and I said to her 'how's the blue tits today missus?'

32: CRITICS are like eunuchs in a harem; they know exactly how it should be done – they see it being done every night, but they cannot do it themselves.

33: THE impact of my play was like the banging together of two damp dish-cloths.

34: GOD created alcohol just to stop the Irish from ruling the world.

35: I HAVE never seen a situation yet so bad that a policeman couldn't make it worse.

36: THE bloody car we went in was only held together by St Christopher medals.

37: A JOB is death without the dignity.

38: HERE'S to the harp of old Ireland, and may it never want for a string as long as there's a gut in a peeler.

39: I FIRST learned the use of whiskey at the age of six from my grandmother who said, 'Give him a sup of it now, and he will never know the taste of it when he grows up', which I suppose is the biggest understatement of all time.

40: WHEN I'm healthy I'm not at all religious, but when I'm sick I'm very religious.

41: HOLY Father, there isn't a man in Dublin that wouldn't go to hell for you.

42: QUEEN Victoria did one good deed during the Irish famine – she gave five pounds to the Relief Fund. But so as not to cause jealousy she gave five pounds on the same day to Battersea Dog's Home.

43: I'M staying alive only to save the funeral expenses.

44: IN jail I had only one brand of tobacco – Three Nuns. None today, none tomorrow and none yesterday.

45: RUMOUR has it that Harry McGill of McGill and Gill publishers, cannot read. In a profession where simple accountancy is preferable to a degree in English, illiteracy is not considered to be a great drawback.

46: THERE are only two reasons for drinking – when you are thirsty, to cure it, and when you are not thirsty to prevent it.

47: LIPS that touch liquor will never touch my liquor.

48: I ALWAYS want one more drink to wash the last one down.

49: THE English, God help them, expect every language to be like their own.

50: CORK people would steal the cross from behind Jesus' back and leave Him hanging in mid-air.

51: WELL, we have one consolation, the condemned man gets the priest and the sacraments, more than his victim got maybe. I venture to suggest that some of them die holier deaths than if they had finished their natural span. But we can't advertise 'Commit a murder and die a happy death'. We'd have them all at it. They take their religion very seriously in Ireland.

52: AN author's first duty is to let down his country.

53: AMERICANS are always boasting about bribery and corruption, as if it was their own special invention, and as if nobody else had any.

54: A MESSAGE in my plays? What the hell do you think I am, a bloody postman?

55: THANK you sister – may you be the mother of a bishop.

56: I'M not a politician – I've got only one face.

57: YES we do have a bath in the house – but thank God we've never had to use it.

58: POUND notes are the best religion in the world.

59: NEVER throw stones at your mother,
You'll be sorry for it when she's dead.
Never throw stones at your mother,
Throw bricks at your father instead.

60: THE way some Civil Servants talk you'd think God was in another department.

61: PORT wine will be supplied to those who are teetotallers, in accordance with the well-known English custom.

62: I DRINK like a fish. The only difference is we drink different stuff.

63: THERE was a fellow in prison whose lawyer was later known to boast that he had got him a suspended sentence. They hanged him.

64: THE only sort of man most women want to marry is the fella with a will of his own – made out in her favour.

65: I ONLY take a drink or two on occasions – when I'm thirsty and when I'm not.

66: NOT all the sins of my past life passed in front of me but as many as could find room in the queue.

67: How's my health? If I felt any better I could not stand it.

68: SHE looked like a woman who looked under her bed hoping to find a man there but only found a collar-stud.

69: IF there were only three Irishmen left in the world, you'd find two of them in a corner talking about the other.

70: SHE was fined for having concealed about her person two Thompson sub-machine guns, three Mills bombs and a stick of dynamite.

✓ 71: SOME people don't like the Irish, but we're very popular among ourselves.

72: I THINK weddings are sadder than funerals because they remind you of your own wedding. You can't be reminded of your own funeral because it hasn't happened.

73: THE English and Americans dislike some Irish – the same Irish that the Irish themselves detest, Irish writers – the ones that think.

74: HE'D drink porter out of a policeman's boots.

75: NEARLY all thieves are Tories. Maybe that's because nearly all Tories are thieves.

76: KILLING your wife is a natural class of a thing that could happen to the best of us.

77: IN prison we sometimes got food with our meals.

78: CORKMEN and Northerners are the hardest to hang; they've such bloody hard necks.

79: IT was a day of rejoicing the day I left school; that was the day the Brothers realised that if you pray long enough your every wish will be God's desire.

80: I WASN'T without ambition in the painting, graining, marbling and lettering game but it was generally accepted that my real talents lay in the placing of bookies' dockets.

81: MY family's land was all in window boxes.

82: A HANGOVER for me is when the brew of the night meets the dawn of the day.

83: THE Irish Navy is the best in the world. Every evening all the sailors can cycle home for their tea.

84: YOU'LL never find high-up civil servants drinking under their own names.

85: THAT man is far too young to have died for Ireland.

86: I ALWAYS carried gelignite; dynamite isn't safe.

87: MY whole system is upset by the sight of a police uniform.

88: I SAY 'bejaysus' a lot because it's only His friends knew him by His first name.

89: THERE was a theologian who saw hell as an empty place but unfortunately for all our peace of minds that was in 1740 – things may well have changed since.

90: IRELAND is a great country to get a letter from.

91: I HAVE forty acres of land in West Clare. When the tide is out.

92: SINCE I was a child, I've had a pathological hatred of country people.

93: ANGLO-IRISHMEN only work at riding horses, drinking whiskey and reading double-meaning books in Irish at Trinity College.

94: WHEN a girl marries in Hollywood she throws the bridegroom away before she throws the bouquet.

95: MY own prejudice is not generally directed against the Swedish people. It wasn't them that caused the Famine.

96: THE number of people who buy books in Ireland would not keep me in drink for the duration of Sunday opening time.

97: POETRY'S all right, but it's all written.

98: WHENEVER you want me to go on television you have only got to say the word – Money.

99: FOR me to praise Shaw or O'Casey would be a piece of impertinence. It would be like praising the lakes of Killarney ... saying they were rather nice looking.

100: THE best words any man can hear at his funeral are 'carry on with the coffin. The corpse'll walk'.

101: ALL marriages are mixed – they're between men and women.

DOMINIC BEHAN

102: THEN one day they opened a Catholic chapel, which was followed by a pub, a block of shops and eventually a school. The school went up last because there was no profit in it.

KATHLEEN BEHAN

103: I WOULDN'T trust my husband with a young woman for five minutes, and he's been dead for twenty-five years.

104: THE neighbours said to me, 'Oh, Mrs Behan, don't go out to Kimmage – that's where they eat their young'.

GEORGE BEST

105: I AM attending Alcoholics Anonymous, but it's difficult to remain anonymous.

GEORGE A. BIRMINGHAM

106: THIS book is dedicated to any friend I have left in Ireland after its publication.

107: HE lied like an eyewitness.

DION BOUCICAULT

108: HOW I wish that Adam had died with all his ribs in his body.

ELIZABETH BOWEN

109: EDITH Sitwell is like a high altar on the move.

TONY BUTLER

110: THE management of an Irish pub cannot be held responsible for any accidents which occur in the mad rush for the doors at closing time.

111: THE Irish climate is wonderful, but the weather ruins it.

112: IN Ireland when the weather forecast is bad, it's invariably correct; when it's good, it's invariably wrong.

PATRICK CAMPBELL

113: FROM my earliest days I have enjoyed an attractive impediment in my speech. I have never permitted the use of the word 'stammer'. I can't say it myself.

114: IN New York it would be absolutely magical if we could alleviate our hunger with something that tasted of food.

115: THE only people I've ever given working orders to have been occasional charwomen, and mostly I've told them not to bother, that I'd do it myself.

RODDY CARR

116: WHEN I roomed with Simon Hobday in South Africa he designated Monday as washday. That meant filling a bath with water, pouring in a liberal amount of detergent, emptying in the entire contents of his suitcase and then proceeding to stir the lot with a putter. When he felt the clothes had been stirred sufficiently, they were thrown out on the balcony to dry.

FRANK CARSON

117: I'M not really a homosexual – I just help them out when they're busy.

118: I USED to sell furniture for a living. The trouble was, it was my own.

119: MY brother has an unusual job. He finds things before other people lose them.

Padraig Colum

120: THE ideal marriage consists of a deaf husband and a blind wife.

Paddy Crosbie

121: IF bullshit was music, that fellow would be a brass band.

John Philpot Curran

122: MY dear doctor, I'm surprised to hear you say that I am coughing very badly, because I have been practising all night.

Michael Davitt

123: YOU are not a proper member of an Irish club until you are barred.

Terence De Vere-White

124: DE Valera discloses the workings of a mind to which incoherence lends an illusion of profundity.

JAMES DILLON

125: MY family was in Irish politics while De Valera's was still bartering budgerigars on the back streets of Barcelona.

JAMES DUFFY

126: THRIFTY! Man, she'd skin a flea for his hide.

MYLES DUNGAN

127: IF David Feherty hadn't been a golfer he probably would have been a wringer-outer for a one-armed window cleaner.

JOHN EGLINGTON

128: CARLETON was a man sent by God in response to the general clamour for an Irish Walter Scott.

DAVID FEHERTY

129: MY golfing partner couldn't hit a tiled floor with a bellyful of puke.

130: COLIN Montgomerie has the temper of a wart-hog recently stung by a wasp and a face like bulldog licking piss off a nettle.

131: JOHN Daly's divots were travelling further than my drives.

DONAL FOLEY

132: A FINE soft day is a day of incessant rain accompanied by a force nine gale.

133: A VETERAN of the War of Independence is the obituary description of every Irishman over 70.

134: HE maintained a delightful formality on social occasions: he always divested himself of his bicycle clips before taking a pint.

135: THOUGH not a formally religious man: he never darkened a church door in his life.

136: HIS charity was legendary: he subscribed to the Herald Boot Fund, 1921.

137: HE was a devoted family man: spends Christmas Day at home.

138: HE was devoted to the sport of Kings: a compulsive gambler.

139: HE contributed generously to church funds: he was a bingo addict.

140: THE statement last week that mortal sins were not being committed any more in Ireland except by a privileged few has prompted a number of old sinners to come together and form an association.

141: DUBLIN was a clear winner in Bord Fáilte's 'Dirty Towns' competition. The strong smell of the Liffey, with its fascinating tang of urine, excreta, rotten dogs and decayed fish sent Dublin into an unassailable lead.

142: THE Dáil has a valuable therapeutic function insofar as it keeps a number of potentially dangerous men off the public streets.

PERCY FRENCH

143: I HAVE just returned from a children's party. I am one of the survivors. There are not many of us.

OLIVER ST JOHN GOGARTY

144: I'M told Bernard Shaw went to church the other day and when they passed him the collection plate he moved aside murmuring 'Press'.

145: NEWGRANGE is described as a pre-Christian cemetery, but this would be misleading except to us who know that the question of subsequent Christianity is unfounded.

146: WHEN St Patrick first visited Ireland there was no word in the Irish language to express sobriety.

147: THERE is no such thing as a large whiskey.

148: IF Evan gave all his reasons for joining the Catholic Church he would be excommunicated.

OLIVER GOLDSMITH

149: ON the stage David Garrick was natural, simple, affecting. It was only when he was off that he was acting.

150: THE man recovered of the bite,
The dog it was that died.

151: I AM told he makes a very handsome corpse and becomes his coffin prodigiously.

152: THERE is nothing so absurd or ridiculous that has not at some time been said by some philosopher.

Michael Hartnett

153: English is the perfect language to sell pigs in.

Father Healy

154: I would prefer Heaven for climate but Hell for society, as all my friends are Protestants.

155: Lunch is a poor compliment to breakfast and an insult to dinner.

John Hume

156: If the word 'No' was removed from the English language, Ian Paisley would be struck speechless.

157: The truth is that Ulster Unionists are loyal not to the crown but to the half crown.

✓158: Anyone who isn't confused in Northern Ireland doesn't really understand what is going on.

159: YOU may certainly not kiss the hand that wrote *Ulysses*. It's done lots of other things as well.

160: BECOME a Protestant? Certainly not. Just because I've lost my faith doesn't mean I've lost my reason.

161: THE only demand I make of my reader is that he should devote his whole life to reading my works.

162: WE have met too late, Mr Yeats; you are too old to be influenced by me.

163: 'WHEN I makes tea I makes tea,' as old mother Grogan said, 'And when I makes water I makes water.'

164: HE is down on his luck at present owing to the mortgaging of his extensive property at Agendath Netaim in faraway Asia Minor, slides of which will now be shown.

165: IRELAND is the only country that never persecuted the Jews – because she never let them in.

166: COME forth Lazarus! And he came fifth and lost the job.

167: I AM a strict teetotaller, not taking anything between drinks.

NORA JOYCE

168: JAMES, why don't you write books that people can read?

PATRICK KAVANAGH

169: THE trees along the banks of the Royal Canal are more sinned against than sinning.

170: THERE are over thirty words in the Irish language which are equivalent to the Spanish 'manana'. But somehow none of them conveys the same sense of urgency.

171: I HAVE just returned from a trip to Paris and let me tell you lads courting in Monaghan is only in its infancy.

EAMON KEANE

172: THE fulminations of the missionaries about sex in Listowel will have as little effect as the droppings of an underweight blackbird on the water level of the Grand Coulee Dam.

173: THERE he goes – the man what learned me English.

174: HE is such a devout Catholic, he won't be happy until he is crucified.

175: GIVEN the unlikely options of attending a funeral or a sex orgy, a true Irishman will always opt for the funeral.

176: THE ultimate role of the Catholic Church in Ireland is the propagation of bingo.

177: I ONCE knew a woman who wore out three bicycles in search of a cure for corns.

178: I WAS entering a hostelry in Killarney when I was approached by a man who accused me of never having written about bucket handles.

179: IN the book of records Dandy Keane was credited with landing the largest enamel chamber pot ever to be hooked by rod and line from one end of the Feale River to the other. I have no idea how many gallons it would contain, but under the entry ran the following description: *Chamber Pot. Enamel. Perforated at bottom. Handle attached. To hold the water of twenty.*

EAMON KELLY

180: 'TIS always a mystery to me how women got on before the looking-glass was invented.

181: WHEN they heard he was from England, they filled him up with every kind of story, for they do enjoy the like.

EDWARD KENEALY

182: WHAT is an Irishman but a mere machine for converting potatoes into human nature?

HUGH LEONARD

183: THERE is only one immutable law in life –
in a gentleman's toilet, incoming traffic has the right of way.

184: DRAMA critics are there to show gay actors what it is like to have a wife.

185: ABSOLUTE equality, that's the thing; and throughout the ages we have always defended to the death the sacred right of every black man, no matter how lowly, to be equal to every other black man.

186: MY grandmother made dying her life's work.

187: ALL I ever seemed to get was the kind of girl who had a special dispensation from the Pope to wear the thickest part of her legs below the knees.

188: THE problem with Ireland is that it is a country full of genius, but with absolutely no talent.

189: AN Irishman will always soften bad news, so that a major coronary is no more than a 'bad turn' and a near-hurricane that leaves thousands homeless is 'good drying weather'.

190: CHICAGO is a city where men are men and the police take Visa.

191: MICHAEL Caine can out-act any – well nearly any – telephone kiosk you care to mention.

192: QUITE simply I am an electric and electronic idiot. Last time I plugged in a table lamp, the life support system in Our Lady's Manor across the road went for its tea and the waiting list shrank to where it became virtually non-existent.

193: HE had a varicose nose and a face like Potato of the Year – the year being 1848.

194: NEVER under any circumstances write comedy for laughs. This is as ruinous as believing that your wife means it when she says: 'Tell me all about her. I swear I don't mind.'

195: FINTAN O'Toole is to theatre what bed-wetting is to nurseries.

196: IF Aer Lingus stopped spending fortunes on advertising, they could afford to use the money saved to improve the services to the degree where they could fulfil the boasts they were no longer making. Got that? No? Never mind, keep taking the ointment.

197: 'Is dona linn an briseadh seo', is RTE speak for 'the cameraman has been taken short'.

DESMOND LYNAM

198: IF you're a sporting star, you're a sporting star. If you don't quite make it you become a coach. If you can't coach, you become a journalist. If you can't spell, you introduce *Grandstand* on a Saturday afternoon.

ROBERT LYND

199: EVERY man of genius is considerably helped by being dead.

Patrick MacGill

200: God is choosy about the company He keeps and never comes near Derry.

Michael MacLiammoir

201: The Irish Republic tonight at midnight. Hilton Edwards piously thanked God that England was free at last from 700 years of Irish domination.

Seumas MacManus

202: It is bad manners to begin courting a widow before she gets home from the funeral.

203: Never make a task of pleasure, as the man said when he dug his wife's grave only three feet deep.

204: There are three things to beware of: the hoof of a horse, the horn of a bull and the smile of an Englishman.

205: Ballygullion girls have a dispensation from the Pope to wear the thick end of their leg downwards.

206: HE was a man of his word and his word was no good.

207: DRYING widows' tears is the most dangerous occupation known to man.

WILLIAM MAGINN

208: THE safety of women consists in one circumstance – men do not possess at the same time the knowledge of thirty-five and the blood of seventeen.

209: A MARRIED woman commonly falls in love with a man as unlike her husband as is possible – but a widow very often marries a man extremely resembling the defunct. The reason is obvious.

210: DON'T marry any woman under twenty; she is not come to her wickedness before that time; nor any woman who has a red nose at any age; because people make observations as you go along the street. 'A cast of the eye' – as the lady casts it on you – may pass muster under some circumstances; and I have even known those who thought it desirable; but absolute squinting is a monopoly of vision which ought not to be tolerated.

211: WHAT the difference between a man and a woman is I cannot conceive.

212: IN Ireland the inevitable never happens but the impossible always does.

213: AN Irish atheist is one who wishes to God he could believe in God.

214: AN Irish bull is always pregnant.

215: NO one ever sank to the depths of evil all at once: it takes forty years to become a Senior Fellow at Trinity College, Dublin.

216: I AM told that Traill is ill. Nothing trivial I hope.

217: BEWARE of French actresses, especially when you are 108.

COUNT MAHONEY

218: I CAN understand Italian, your Majesty, if it's spoken in Irish.

EDWARD MARTYN

219: GEORGE Moore suffered from mental diarrhoea which had to be shot all over his friends.

SPIKE MILLIGAN

220: MONEY can't buy you happiness, but it does bring you a more pleasant form of misery.

221: To duplicate the taste of a hammer-head shark, boil old newspapers in Sloan's Liniment.

222: I THOUGHT I would begin by reading a poem by Shakespeare, but, then I thought 'Why should I?' He never reads any of mine.

223: TELL your mummies and daddies to buy this book and hit them until they do.

224: IT was the perfect Irish marriage – she didn't want to and he couldn't.

225: I HAVE the body of an eighteen year old. I keep it in the fridge.

226: A SURE cure for seasickness is to sit under a tree.

227: Is there anything worn under the kilt? No, it's all in perfect working order.

228: My army medical consisted of two questions (i) Have you got piles? (ii) Is there any insanity in your family? I answered yes to both and was accepted A1.

229: My father had a profound influence on me – he was a lunatic.

230: His vibrato sounded like he was driving a tractor over ploughed fields with weights tied to his scrotum.

231: For breakfast, the first morning I was in France, I had porridge and frogs washed down with a steaming bidet of coffee.

232: I went to Paris and stayed at the Hotel Demolition by Kirkpatrick.

233: I shook hands with a friendly Arab – I still have my right hand to prove it.

234: In India, a farm hand was caught in the act with his cow. He said he had bad eyesight and thought it was his wife.

235: I'm not Jewish – it's just that this tree fell on me.

236: DON'T stand around doing nothing – people will think you're just a workman.

237: SOME people are always late, like the late King George the Fifth.

238: READY, fire, aim.

239: MONEY can't buy friends but you can get a better class of enemy.

240: THE Army works like this: if a man dies when you hang him, keep hanging him until he gets used to it.

241: EVERY night, when my father comes home, he gets out a pistol and shouts, 'Hitler! If you're in this house, come out with your hands up'.

242: SHE set out the alarm for seven but there were only two of us.

243: THE public of dear old England has been coaxed into giving £350,000 towards buying a Leonardo cartoon which was in 'danger' of being bought abroad (up until then it had been kept in a cellar).

244: THERE are no advantages to being a tax exile domiciled in Ireland. What you save on tax, you spend on drink.

245: HE had a brain that would have fitted in a thimble with room to spare.

246: WE were issued with seasickness pills. I never suffer from this so I threw them over the side, where the fish ate them, and were immediately sick.

GEORGE MOORE

247: OSCAR Wilde paraphrased and inverted the witticisms and epigrams of others. His method of literary piracy was on the lines of the robber Cacus, who dragged stolen cows backwards by the tails to his cavern so that their hoofprints might not lead to detection.

248: IN Ireland a girl has the choice between perpetual virginity and perpetual pregnancy.

249: DON'T touch a woman's knee at the dinner table. She has an instinctive knowledge whether a man who touches her knee is caressing her or only wiping his greasy fingers on her stocking.

250: I ATTRIBUTE my long and healthy life to the fact that I never touched a cigarette, a drink, or a girl until I was ten years old.

251: IF I was to write Diarmuid and Grainne in French; Lady Gregory would then translate my French into English; O'Donoghue would then translate the English into Irish and then Lady Gregory would translate the Irish into English! After that Yeats would put style on it.

252: ALL reformers are bachelors.

253: THE real genius for love lies not in getting into, but getting out of love.

254: IT does not matter how badly you paint as long as you don't paint badly like other people.

255: AT 46 or thereabouts one begins to feel that one's time for love is over; one is consultant rather than practitioner.

256: THERE is nothing so consoling as to find that one's neighbour's troubles are at least as great as one's own.

THOMAS MOORE

257: 'COME, come,' said Tom's father,
   'At your time of life,
   There's no longer excuse
   For thus playing the rake.
   It is time you should think boy,

Of taking a wife.'
'Why so it is father –
Whose wife shall I take?'

EAMON NALLY

258: AN Irish politician is a man of few words but he uses them often.

259: BORD Fáilte road signs are ignorance embossed in cast iron.

260: THERE has been another revolution in South America. But then it's Tuesday isn't it?

MICHAEL NEARY

261: WHEN primitive man beat the ground with sticks, they called it witchcraft. When modern man does the same thing they call it golf.

CONOR CRUISE O'BRIEN

262: YOU are not an agnostic, Paddy. You are just a fat slob who is too lazy to go to mass.

263: A SOCIALIST is a Protestant variety of communist.

264: THE right to pay fees to lawyers is a fundamental and ancient human right, and is at the kernel of what we know as democracy.

265: THE typical west of Ireland family consists of father, mother, twelve children and resident Dutch anthropologist.

266: PEOPLE who spend most of their natural lives riding iron bicycles over the rocky roads of this parish get their personalities mixed up with the personalities of their bicycles, as a result of the interchanging of the atoms of each of them and you would be surprised at the number of people in these parts who are nearly half people and half bicycles.

267: HAVING considered the matter in – of course – all its aspects, I have decided that there is no excuse for poetry. Poetry gives no adequate return for money, is expensive to print by reason of the waste of space occasioned by its form, and nearly always promulgates illusory concepts of life. But a better case for the banning of all poetry is the simple fact that most of it is bad. Nobody is going to manufacture a thousand tons of jam in the expectation that five tons may be eatable. Furthermore, poetry has the effect on the negligible handful who read it of stimulating them to write poetry themselves. One poem, if widely disseminated, will breed perhaps a thousand inferior cases.

268: MOST of the cost of a pint of Guinness is tax; most of the tax is spent on the dole; and most of the dole goes on Guinness.

269: OUR ancestors believed in magic, prayers, trickery, browbeating and bullying: I think it would be fair to sum that list up as 'Irish politics'.

270: THE brother bars the doctors. He'd die roarin' before he'd let them boys put a finger on him. And of course half the pills he does be swallyin' is poison. Poison, man. Anybody else takin' so many pills as the brother would be gone to the wall years ago. But the brother's health stands up to it. Because do you know he's a man with an iron constitution.

271: THE brother opened Charley in 1934. He gave Charley's kidneys a thorough overhaul, and that's a game none of your doctors would try their hand at. He had Charley in the bathroom for five hours. Nobody was let in, of course, but the water was goin' all the time and all classes of cut throats been sharpened, you could hear your man workin' at the strap. O a great night's work.

272: WHISKEY puts a lining like leather on the stomach, a man from Balbriggan was telling me.

273: HE would take inverted commas from no man.

274: THIS is a very hardened character your honour. He was convicted for loitering at Swansea in 1933.

275: DOUBLE You Bee Yeats once said to me.

276: A POPULAR figure in Irish dancing circles, he was a firm believer in the immutable principles laid down by the Manchester school.

277: OUR sole musical tradition is bound up with blind harpers, tramps with home made fiddles, Handel in Fish-handel street, John McCormack praising our airport, and no street in the whole capital named after John Field.

In the great gombeen metropolis of 'our land', art is the one thing that your newly-emancipated peasant finds irresistible; even after two generations he is still flabbergasted at the idea of seeing books that are not almanacs, pictures that are not given away with Christmas numbers of religious periodicals and drink that is not lethal two-year old Irish.

278: IT cannot too often be pointed out that women are people.

279: IT cannot be too often repeated that I am not for sale. I was bought in 1921 and the transaction was final and conclusive.

280: IT has been held that the teaching of subjects other than fishing not through Irish but through the medium of Irish leads to a generation 'illiterate in two languages'.

SEAN O'CASEY

281: I NEVER heard him cursing; I don't believe he was ever drunk in his life – sure he's not like a Christian at all.

282: I'M telling you Joxer, the whole world's in a terrible state of chassis.

283: P. G. WODEHOUSE is the performing flea of English literature.

DANIEL O'CONNELL

284: HE had all the characteristics of a poker except its occasional warmth.

285: PEEL'S smile is like the silver fittings on a coffin.

Sean O'Faolain

286: An Irish queer is a fellow who prefers women to drink.

287: I have only four plausible reasons for Irish continence: that sexual desire is sublimated by religion, exhausted by sport, drugged by drink or deflected by either an innate or inculcated Puritanism.

288: Did it ever occur to you that the bottom of a whiskey bottle is much too near the top?

289: All Corkmen have a hard streak in them. The gentlest are the most cruel. All are cynics. The smilers are the worst.

290: A true Irishman is a fellow who would trample over the bodies of twelve naked woman to reach a pint of porter.

Kevin O'Higgins

291: When I think of the hardship involved in having only seven hours to drink on a Sunday, my soul shudders.

Tony O'Reilly

292: Horrocks-Taylor came towards me with the ball. Horrocks went one way, Taylor went the other and I was left holding the hyphen.

Shamus O'Shamus

293: Cork, like Dublin, possesses a river, but there is no record that any Cork townsman has ever succeeded in spitting across it. That is not to say that the townsmen of Cork have given up trying. Indeed, some Cork townsmen endeavour to keep themselves in practice even when their beautiful river is not in sight.

294: A complete description of Belfast is given by: Population 200,000; early closing day Wednesday.

Peter O'Toole

 295: I'm not crazy, but I think everyone else is.

296: I am the only man in the world where both my first and second names are synonyms for 'penis'.

Ian Paisley

297: WHO is King Billy? Go home man and read your Bible.

298: I HAVE reason to believe that the fowl pest outbreaks are the work of the IRA.

299: THE RUC do not assault anyone at a republican parade unless they see fit.

300: THE Catholics have been interfering in Ulster affairs since 1641.

Charles Stewart Parnell

301: GENTLEMEN, it seems unanimous that we cannot agree.

Maureen Potter

302: ASSUMPTA, take your foot out of your mouth, it's a fast day.

303: CHRISTY, look at the ink you've spilled on that tablecloth and your father has't even read it yet.

304: O LIST to the tale of a poor Irish harpist,
Who plays every night in hotel cabaret.
She plucks the strings quietly,
She sings so politely,
But all of those tourists keep guzzling away.
She sings of the famine,
While they're knocking back salmon,
Paté de foie gras and lobster mayonnaise.
But this hungry Gael Linner,
Can't have her own dinner,
'Til she sings her sad song of
The dark penal days.

305: SOME Irish drinkers won't take a bath unless it has a head on it.

306: YOU'RE not supposed to look happy doing an Irish dance.

307: As the Dublin woman said when she saw the Leaning Tower of Pisa, 'willya looka, it's crooka'.

SARAH PURSER

308: SOME men kiss and tell; George Moore tells but doesn't kiss.

309: ALL these people with wooden legs – it's pathetic, they're not fooling anyone.

310: PEOPLE often say to me 'What are you doing in my garden?'

BOYLE ROACH

311: No man can be in two places at the one time unless he is a bird.

312: THE man who would stoop so low as to write an anonymous letter, the least he might do is to sign his name to it.

313: WE put them all to the sword; not a soul of them escaped alive except some that were drowned in the adjoining bog.

314: THE only living beasts on the farms of Ireland are the birds that fly over them.

315: MANY hundreds of people are destitute even of the very goods they possess.

316: IRON gates will last forever and afterwards they can be used for making horse shoes.

317: I ANSWERED in the affirmative with an emphatic 'No!'

318: BY trial of jury I have lived and please God with trial by jury I shall die.

319: THREE-QUARTERS of what the opposition says about us is lies and the other half is without any foundation in truth.

320: MISTER Speaker, the country is in such a desperate state that little children, who can neither walk nor talk, are running around the streets cursing their maker.

321: THE present tax on shoe leather is putting an intolerable burden on the bare-footed peasantry of Ireland.

322: I WOULD give up half – nay, the whole of the constitution to preserve the remainder.

323: SINGLE misfortunes rarely come alone and the worst of all misfortunes is usually followed by a greater misfortune.

324: THE only way of preventing what is past is to put a stop to it before it happens.

325: THE cup of Ireland's miseries has been overflowing for centuries, but it is not yet full.

326: I STAND here, neither partial nor impartial.

327: HALF the lies our opponents tell about us are not true.

328: I SHOULD have answered your letter a fortnight ago, but I didn't receive it until this morning.

329: WHILE I write this I hold a sword in one hand and a pistol in the other.

HAL ROACH

330: HAVE you been to Donegal? What a town. You plug in your shaver and the street lights dim.

331: THE weather in Cork is something else. It's the only place in the world you can wake up in the morning and hear the birds coughing.

GEORGE RUSSELL

332: A LITERARY movement is five or six people who live in the same town and hate each other.

333: WHICH painting in the National Gallery would I save if there was a fire? The one nearest the door of course.

334: HE who can does – he who cannot, teaches.

335: THERE is nothing on earth intended for innocent people, so horrible as a school. It is in some respects more cruel than a prison. In a prison you are not forced to read books written by the warders and the governor.

336: ONLY lawyers and mental defectives are automatically exempt from jury duty.

337: TWO people getting together to write a book is like three people getting together to have a baby. One of them is superfluous.

338: NATURE, not content with denying him the art of thinking, conferred on him the gift of writing.

339: I CAN forgive Alfred Nobel for having invented dynamite, but only a fiend in human form could have invented the Nobel prize.

340: In Ireland they try to make a cat clean by rubbing its nose in its own filth. James Joyce has tried the same treatment on the human subject. I hope it may prove successful.

341: I often quote myself. It adds spice to my conversations.

342: Condemned female murderers get sheaves of offers of marriage.

343: When we want to read about the deeds that are done for love, whither do we turn? To the murder columns.

344: A woman waits motionless until she is wooed. That is how the spider waits for the fly.

345: Communism is the lay form of Catholicism.

346: I was always unlawful; I broke the law when I was born because my parents weren't married.

347: Go on writing plays my boy. One of these days a London producer will go into his office and say to his secretary. 'Is there a play from Shaw this morning?' and when she says 'No' he will say, 'Well, then we'll have to start on the rubbish.' And that's your chance my boy.

348: Am I Shaw? I am positive.

349: I HATE the poor and look forward eagerly to their extermination.

350: THE English churchgoer prefers a severe preacher because he thinks a few home truths will do his neighbour no harm.

351: PATRIOTISM is your conviction that your country is superior to all others because you were born in it.

352: How can what an Englishman believes be heresy? It is a contradiction in terms.

353: IF I had my life to live over again I should devote it to the establishment of some arrangement of headphones and microphones or the like whereby the noises used by musical maniacs should be audible to themselves only. It should be made a felony to play a musical instrument in any other than a completely soundproof room.

354: AN Englishman thinks he is being moral when he is only being uncomfortable.

355: FIRST love is only a little foolishness and a lot of curiosity. No really self-respecting woman would take advantage of it.

356: DRINK is the curse of my unhappy country. I take it myself because I have a weak heart and a poor digestion; but in principle I'm a teetotaller.

357: THE man that is not prejudiced against a horse-thief is not fit to sit on a jury in this town.

358: VENUS, a beautiful good-natured lady, was the goddess of love; Juno, a terrible shrew, the goddess of marriage; and they were always mortal enemies.

359: No man is a match for a woman except with a poker and a pair of hobnailed boots.

360: MARRIAGE will always be a popular institution, because it combines a maximum of temptation with a maximum of opportunity.

361: I HAVE a beard because I have written several plays in the time I would have spent shaving.

362: THE more things a man is ashamed of, the more respectable he is.

363: IF all economists were laid end to end, they would not reach a conclusion.

364: NOBEL Prize money is a lifebelt thrown to a swimmer who has already reached the shore safely.

365: A NEWSPAPER is a device which is unable to discriminate between a bicycle accident and the collapse of civilisation.

366: I AM the most spontaneous man in the world because every word, every gesture, and every retort has been carefully rehearsed.

367: HE knows nothing and thinks he knows everything. That points clearly to a political career.

368: GAMES are for people who can neither read nor think.

369: WHEN you find some country gentleman keeping up the old English customs at Christmas and so forth, who is he? An American who has just bought the place.

370: AN Englishman is at his best on the links, and at his worst in the Cabinet.

371: THAT is the whole secret of successful fighting. Get your enemy at a disadvantage; and never, on any account, fight him on equal terms.

372: WHEN men die of disease they are said to die of natural causes. When they recover (and they mostly do) the doctor gets the credit for curing them.

373: NOTHING soothes me more after a long and maddening course of piano recitals than to sit and have my teeth drilled.

374: YOU can always tell an old soldier by the inside of his holsters and cartridge boxes. The young ones carry pistols and cartridges: the old ones, grub.

375: THE British soldier can stand up to anything – except the British War Office.

376: THERE is no love sincerer than the love of food.

377: AT every one of those concerts in England you will find rows of weary people who are there, not because they really like classical music but because they think they ought to like it.

378: THERE is no satisfaction in hanging a man who does not object to it.

379: THERE is nothing so bad or so good that you will not find Englishmen doing it; but you will never find an Englishman in the wrong. He does everything on principle. He fights you on patriotic principles; he robs you on business principles; he enslaves you on imperial principles; he supports his king on royal principles and cuts off his king's head on republican principles.

380: LORD Roseberry was a man who never missed an occasion to let slip an opportunity.

381: ENGLAND and America are two countries separated by the same language.

382: DANCING is a perpendicular expression of a horizontal desire.

383: WE were not fairly beaten. No Englishman is ever fairly beaten.

384: A DRAMA critic is a man who leaves no turn unstoned.

385: IRISH Protestantism is not a religion. It is a class prejudice, a conviction that Roman Catholics are socially inferior persons who will go to Hell when they die and leave Heaven in the exclusive possession of Protestant ladies and gentlemen.

386: THE ideal love affair is one conducted by post. My correspondence with Ellen Terry was a wholly satisfactory love affair. She got tired of five husbands; but she never got tired of me.

387: WOMEN want other women's husbands like horse-thieves prefer a horse that is broken in to one that is wild.

388: A MAN should have one woman to prevent him thinking too much about women in general.

389: THE only man who had a proper understanding of Parliament was old Guy Fawkes.

390: A BRIGAND lives by robbing the rich: a gentleman by robbing the poor.

391: VERY nice sort of place, Oxford, I should think, for people who like that sort of place.

392: I AM somewhat surprised to hear a Roman Catholic quote so essentially a Protestant document as the Bible.

393: MY first doubt as to whether God could really be a good Protestant was suggested by the fact that the best voices available for combination with my mother's in the works of the great composers had been unaccountably vouchsafed to Roman Catholics.

394: A BUSINESSMAN is someone to whom age brings golf instead of wisdom.

395: I HAVE never thought much of the courage of the lion-tamer; inside the cage he is at least safe from other men.

JIM SHERIDAN

396: THERE'S a great saying in Ireland, and it's not without irony. It says that the last time we played England we beat them one–all.

JOHN D. SHERIDAN

397: THE first rule of hospitality is that the visitor must never get a glimpse of the conditions in which you normally live.

398: MARROWS, the gardening book told me, were gross feeders, but this was putting it mildly, for those marrows of mine ate not only the manure but all of the rubble and some of the concrete. One of them, I could almost swear, ate an old zinc bucket.

399: I AM always welcome in a poker school, since my face is an emotional barometer, and any good player can tell by looking at me whether I am holding two small pairs or a broken flush. But when I look at a good poker player I have difficulty in deciding whether he is dead or alive.

400: I READ where an ape has been taught to speak two words of English – when he learns ninety-eight more he can go to Hollywood and become a producer.

401: MY soccer career was brief and inglorious. I played in only one match, and scored a goal with a brilliant left-footed drive that gave our goalkeeper no chance.

402: WHAT prompted me to take up writing? Well, in the first place, the sandwich-board used to chafe me.

403: WHEN you send an article to the editor of a newspaper, it is a mistake to number the pages. Send them in a jumble, and if they do not come back in the proper order you will know that the editor did not even read the thing.

404: ONCE a woman has decided to knit a jersey, nothing short of total paralysis will stop her.

405: THIS book is dedicated to whom it may concern.

406: FROM the silence that prevails, I conclude that Lauderdale has been telling a joke.

407: IT is not in my interest to pay the principal nor in my principle to pay the interest.

408: THE right honourable gentleman is indebted to his memory for his jests, and to his imagination for his facts.

409: A LIMERICK banker had an iron leg and it was the softest thing about him.

410: MY honourable friend has just gone to London with a shirt and a guinea and he'll not change either until he comes back.

411: ONE would as soon make love to the Archbishop of Canterbury as to Mrs Siddons.

412: WHEN a heroine goes mad, she always goes into white satin.

413: SHE is as headstrong as an allegory on the banks of the Nile.

414: I WOULD rather choose a wife of mine to have the usual number of limbs, and although one eye may be very agreeable, the prejudice has always run in favour of two.

415: WHEN she has finished painting her face she joins it on so badly to her neck that she looks like a mended statue.

416: WHEN my son Tom announced that he would proclaim his independence of party as an MP by writing the words TO LET on his forehead, I advised him to write underneath, UNFUR-NISHED.

JAMES STEPHENS

417: MEN come of age at sixty, women at sixteen.

418: SLEEP is an excellent way of listening to the opera.

JONATHAN SWIFT

419: A TAVERN is a place where they sell madness by the bottle.

420: IF a lump of soot falls into the soup, and you cannot conveniently get it out, stir it well in, and it will give the soup a French taste.

421: BRING not a bagpipe to a man in trouble.

422: No man is thoroughly miserable unless he is condemned to live in Ireland.

423: I PROPOSE that a tax be levied on female beauty. Let every woman be permitted to assess her own charms – then she'll be generous enough.

424: NEVER remark in England that the air in Ireland is healthy and excellent or they will most certainly tax it.

425: IF the Church and the devil went to law the devil would win for all the lawyers and attorneys would be on his side.

426: I AM almost done with harridans, and shall soon become old enough to fall in love with girls of fourteen.

427: I NEVER knew any man in my life who could not bear another's misfortune perfectly like a Christian.

428: HE had been eight years upon a project for extracting sunbeams out of cucumbers, which were to be put into phials hermetically sealed and let out to warm the air in raw inclement summers.

429: UNDER an oak in stormy weather;
   I joined this rogue and whore together;
   And none but he who rules the thunder
   Can pull this rogue and whore asunder.

430: WHY, every one as they like; as the good
   woman said when she kissed her cow.

431: FAITH, that's as well said, as if I had said it myself.

432: YOU have a head, and so has a pin.

433: NEVER lie to your master or mistress, unless
   you have some hopes that they cannot find it
   out.

434: A MAN who had a mind to sell his house, carried a piece of brick in his pocket, which he
   showed as a pattern to encourage purchasers.

435: I HAVE been assured by a very knowing American of my acquaintance in London that a
   healthy young child, well nursed, is at a year
   old a most delicious, nourishing and whole-
   some food, whether steamed, roasted, baked
   or boiled: and I make no doubt that it will
   equally serve in a fricassee or a ragout.

436: ALL political parties die of swallowing their own
   lies.

437: A VERY little wit is valued in a woman, as we are pleased with a few words spoken plain by a parrot.

438: SERVANTS never come till you have been called three or four times or more, for none but dogs will come at the first whistle; and when the master calls, 'Who's there?', no servant is bound to come; for who's there is nobody's name.

DENNIS TAYLOR

439: ALEX Higgins should have been here today, but he was launching a ship in Belfast and they couldn't get him to let go of the bottle.

440: THEY say the situation in Northern Ireland is not as bad as they say it is.

NIALL TOIBIN

441: THE true Dubliner is a man who can peel an orange in his pocket.

442: A CORKMAN can be homesick even when he is a home.

443: A CAVAN farmer, to cover the possibility of sudden unexpected visitors, can often be found eating his dinner from a drawer.

444: PEOPLE from the Irish Midlands are often described as 'phlegmatic' which is another word for 'thick'.

445: OF course Cork people will buy Irish goods. Provided they are made in Cork.

446: IRELAND, the geographers tell us, is an island three hundred miles long and a hundred and fifty miles thick.

447: AN Irishman is just a machine for turning Guinness into urine, which as any Murphy's drinker will tell you is a superfluous exercise anyway.

JOE TOMELTY

448: IF there is music in Hell it will be bagpipes.

GEORGE TYRRELL

449: A TEMPERANCE Hotel! You might as well talk about a celibate brothel.

450: I NEVER quite forgave Mahaffy for getting himself suspended from preaching in the College Chapel. Ever since his sermons were discontinued, I suffer from insomnia in church.

Duke of Wellington

451: I DON'T know what effect those men will have
on the enemy, but, by God, they terrify me.

452: I CAN only hope that when the enemy reads the
list of my officers' names he trembles as I do.

453: JUST because a racehorse is born in a pigsty,
that does not make him a pig.

454: GOD save the Queen, and may all your wives
be like her.

455: THE Irish militia are useless in times of war,
and dangerous in times of peace.

456: WE always have been, we are and I hope that
we always shall be, detested in France.

Oscar Wilde

457: THE only thoroughly original ideas I have ever
heard Mr Whistler express have had reference
to his superiority as a painter over painters
greater than himself.

458: MR Whistler, with all his faults, was never
guilty of writing a line of poetry.

459: WHEN I was young I used to think that money was the most important thing in life. Now that I am old, I know it is.

460: IT is only by not paying one's bills that one can hope to live in the memory of the commercial classes.

461: WORK is the curse of the drinking classes.

462: IGNORANCE is like a delicate exotic fruit; touch it and the bloom is gone.

463: WHENEVER cannibals are on the brink of starvation, Heaven, in its infinite mercy, sends them a fat missionary.

464: TELL the cook of this restaurant with my compliments that these are the very worst sandwiches in the whole world, and that, when I ask for a watercress sandwich, I do not mean a loaf with a field in the middle of it.

465: I OFTEN take exercise. Why only yesterday I had breakfast in bed.

466: I NEVER travel without my diary. One should always have something sensational to read on the train.

467: I WAS working on the proofs of one of my poems all day. In the morning I put a comma in and in the afternoon I took it back out again.

468: I'VE given up reading books. I find it takes my mind off myself.

469: THERE are two ways of disliking poetry. One way is to dislike it and the other is to read Pope.

470: THIS book of Italian literature shows a want of knowledge that must be the result of years of study.

471: ONE should not be too severe on English novels; they are the only relaxation of the intellectually unemployed.

472: *ANDIATOROCTE* is the title of a volume of poems by the Rev. Clarence Walworth of Albany, N.Y. It is a word borrowed from the Indians and should, we think, be returned to them as soon as possible.

473: THE General was essentially a man of peace – except of course in his domestic affairs.

474: To lose one parent may be regarded as a misfortune; to lose both looks like carelessness.

475: THERE is nothing in the world like the devotion of a married woman. It's a thing no married man knows anything about.

476: NIAGARA Falls is the bride's second great disappointment.

477: WOMEN have a much better time than men in this world. There are far more things forbidden to them.

478: WOMEN love men for their defects; if men have enough of them, women will forgive them everything, even their gigantic intellects.

479: DAMMIT, sir, it is your duty to get married. You can't always be living for pleasure.

480: POOR old Lord Mortlake, who had only two topics of conversation; his gout and his wife. I never could quite make out which of the two he was talking about.

481: PLEASE do not shoot the pianist – he is doing his best.

482: YOU must play Chopin to me. The man with whom my wife ran away played Chopin exquisitely.

483: Of course America had often been discovered before Columbus, but it had always been hushed up.

484: I HAVE to choose between this world, the next world and Australia.

485: As for marriage, it is one of America's most popular institutions. The American man marries early and the American woman marries often; and they get on extremely well together.

486: Know him? I know him so well that we haven't spoken to each other for over ten years.

487: Always forgive your enemies. Nothing annoys them so much.

488: If this is the way that Queen Victoria treats her prisoners, she doesn't deserve to have any.

489: I must decline your invitation owing to an engagement I am just about to make.

490: It is perfectly monstrous the way people go about nowadays saying things against one, behind one's back, that are absolutely and entirely true.

491: I ALWAYS pass on good advice – it's the only thing one can do with it.

492: IT is very easy to endure the difficulties of one's enemies. It is the successes of one's friends that are hard to bear.

493: FRANK Harris has been invited to every great house in England – once.

494: I CAN resist everything except temptation.

495: FASHION is a form of ugliness so intolerable that we have to alter it every six months.

496: I LIVE in terror of not being misunderstood.

497: YOU should study the Peerage; it is the best thing in fiction the English have ever done.

498: THE extraordinary thing about the lower classes in England is that they are always losing their relations. They are extremely fortunate in that respect.

499: THE English country gentleman galloping after a fox – the unspeakable in pursuit of the uneatable.

500: A CIGARETTE is the perfect type of a perfect pleasure. It is exquisite and leaves one quite un-
satisfied. What more can one want?

501: THIRTY-FIVE is a very attractive age. London
society is full of women who have of their own
free choice remained thirty-five for years.

502: FOOTBALL is all very well a good game for rough
girls, but not for delicate boys.

503: ONE should always play fairly when one has
the winning cards.

504: I NEVER play cricket. It requires one to assume
such indecent postures.

505: THE play was a great success, but the audience
was a disaster.

506: THE central problem in Hamlet is whether the
critics are mad or only pretending to be mad.

507: A PLAGIARIST is a writer of plays.

508: I CAN believe anything as long as it is incredi-
ble.

509: A GENTLEMAN never insults anyone unintention-
ally.

510: ONE can survive anything nowadays except death and live down anything except a good reputation.

511: THE English public takes no interest in a work of art until it is told that the work in question is immoral.

512: IF one hears bad music it is one's duty to drown it by one's conversation.

513: I DON'T want money. It is only people who pay their bills who want money and I never pay mine.

514: MEREDITH is a prose Browning, and so is Browning.

515: THERE is only one thing worse than being talked about and that is not being talked about.

516: WHEN you are alone with Max Beerbohm, he takes off his face and reveals his mask.

517: HE knew the precise psychological moment when to say nothing.

518: WHEN I was your age I had been an inconsolable widower for three months, and was already paying my addresses to your admirable mother.

519: WHEN I went to America, I had two secretaries – one for autographs, the other for locks of hair. Within six months the one had died of writer's cramp, the other was completely bald.

520: LONG engagements give people the opportunity of finding out each other's character before marriage, which is never advisable.

521: AN engagement is hardly a serious one that has not been broken off at least once.

522: I SOMETIMES think that God in creating man somewhat overestimated His ability.

523: IT is only an auctioneer who can equally and impartially admire all schools of art.

524: I HATE vulgar realism in literature. The man who would call a spade a spade should be compelled to use one. It is the only thing he is fit for.

525: BERNARD Shaw is an excellent man; he has not an enemy in the world and none of his friends like him.

526: IT is always a silly thing to give advice but to give good advice is fatal.

527: BAD artists always admire each other's work; they call it being broadminded and free from prejudice.

528: THE advantage of the emotions is that they lead us astray.

529: FRIENDSHIP is far more tragic than love. It lasts longer.

530: PUNCTUALITY is the thief of time.

531: I HAVE nothing to declare except my genius.

532: GEORGE Moore wrote excellent English until he discovered grammar.

533: To win back my youth there is nothing I won't do – except to take exercise, get up early and be a useful member of the community.

534: I DON'T at all like knowing what people say of me behind my back. It makes me far too conceited.

535: MEREDITH! Who can define him? His style is chaos illuminated by flashes of lightning. As a writer he has mastered everything except language: as a novelist he can do everything except tell a story. As an artist he is everything, except articulate.

536: BEING natural is only a pose, and the most irritating pose I know.

537: IN England, at any rate, education produces no effect whatsoever. If it did, it would prove a serious danger to the upper classes, and would probably lead to acts of violence in Grosvenor Square.

538: IF one tells the truth, one is sure, sooner or later, to be found out.

539: IN examinations, the foolish ask questions that the wise cannot answer.

540: THE old believe everything: the middle-aged suspect everything: the young know everything.

541: EVERYBODY who is incapable of learning has taken to teaching.

542: MORALITY is simply the attitude we adopt towards people whom we personally dislike.

543: IN married life, three is company and two is none.

544: UNTRUTHFUL! My nephew, Algernon? Impossible! He is an Oxonian.

545: No woman should ever be quite accurate about her age. It looks so calculating.

546: No good deed ever goes unpunished.

547: I HEAR her hair has turned quite gold from grief.

548: A TYPEWRITER, when played with expression, is no more annoying than a piano.

JOHN WINSTANLEY

549: CRIES Celia to a reverend dean
   'What reason can be given
   Since marriage is a holy thing,
   That there are none in heaven?'

   'There are no women', he replied;
   She quick returned the jest;
   'Women there are, but I'm afraid,
   They cannot find a priest.'

W. B. YEATS

550: I AM not feeling very well. I can only write prose today.

551: SOME people say there is a God; others say there is no God. The truth probably lies somewhere in between.

552: THE only trouble with Seamus O'Sullivan is that when he's not drunk he's sober.

JOHN BUTLER YEATS

553: A MAN who understands one woman is qualified to understand pretty well everything.

INDEX

A

Absence: 19
Actresses: 217
Adam: 108
Advice: 491, 526
Aer Lingus: 196
Age: 501, 540, 545
Agnostics: 262
Agreement: 301
Alarm: 242
America: 26, 53, 483, 519
Americans: 369
Anglo-Irishmen: 93
Animals: 453
Answers: 317
Arabs: 233
Army: 228, 240
Art: 243, 254, 333, 511, 523, 527
Australia: 484

B

Banking: 407
Bachelors: 252
Bath: 57
Beerbohm, Max: 516
Belief: 508
Belfast: 28, 294
Bicycles: 177, 266

Bible: 29, 297, 392
Birds: 311
Bookies: 80
Books: 96, 106, 159, 161, 168, 223, 337, 405, 468
Bord Fáilte: 259
Brains: 245
Britain: 15
Browning; Robert: 514
Business: 460

C

Caine, Michael: 191
Cards: 503
Cars: 36
Carleton, William: 128
Cavan: 443
Chamber Pots: 179
Charity: 136
Chassis: 282
Chicago: 190
Children: 320, 435
Church: 450
Cigarettes: 500
Clocks: 12
Clubs: 123
Colours: 3
Comedy: 194

Football: 396, 401, 502
France: 231, 232, 456
Friendship: 486, 529
Funerals: 100, 175, 202
Furniture: 118

G

Gambling: 138
Games: 368
Gardens: 310, 398, 399
Garrick, David: 149
Gates: 316
Gentlemen: 509
Genius: 199, 531
Girls: 187, 205, 248
God: 522, 551
Golf: 116, 127, 129, 130,
    131, 261, 394
Graveyards: 22
Grief: 547

H

Hamlet: 506
Hanging: 378
Harris, Frank: 493
Hatred: 92
Heads: 432
Headstrong: 413
Health: 67, 225, 250, 270,
    271
Heroines: 412

Hollywood: 94, 400
Homosexuals: 117
House: 434
Humour: 5

I

Ignorance: 462
Illness: 216
India: 234
Interviews: 16
Inverted commas: 273
Invitations: 489
IRA: 298
Ireland: 90, 188, 212, 422,
    424, 446
Irish: 27, 69, 71, 73, 280
Irish bulls: 214
Irish language: 190
Italian: 218

J

Jews: 165, 235
Jobs: 37, 119
Jokes: 406
Joyce, James: 340
Juries: 318, 336, 357

K

Killarney: 178
Kilts: 227
Kissing: 430